A to Z Brazil

BY JUSTINE AND RON FONTES

children's press®
A Division of Scholastic Inc.
New York Toronto London Auckland Sydney
Mexico City New Delhi Hong Kong
Danbury, Connecticut

Consultant: Adriana Dominguez
Series Design: Marie O'Neill
Photo Research: Candlepants Incorporated

The photos on the cover show a Bahian sculpture (right), a toucan (bottom), a boy with a monkey (middle), and giant water lilies (left).

Photographs © 2003: AP/Wide World Photos: 35 left; Archive Photos/Getty Images: 38 top; Corbis Images: 12 bottom, 13 right (AFP), cover top right, 13 left, 14 (Archivo Iconografico, SA), 10 right, 16 right, 18 bottom, 24 right (Ricardo Azoury), 15 right (Bettmann), 10 left (Jonathan Blair), 25 center (Jan Butchofsky-Houser), 32 (Carpenter Collection), 15 left (Christie's Images), 5 bottom, 34 bottom (Michael & Patricia Fogden), 9 right, 31, 34 top (Owen Franken), 8 bottom (Arvind Garg), 4 top, 19 left (Wolfgang Kaehler), 16 left, 25 top, 25 bottom, 28 top, 37 bottom (Stephanie Maze), 35 bottom right (Joe McDonald), 8 top, 29 (Viviane Moos), 19 right (NASA), 7 (Premium Stock), 35 top right (Reuter NewMedia Inc.), 34 inset (Kevin Schafer), 26 (Staffan Wildstrand), 6 bottom (Peter M. Wilson), 12 top, 38 inset; Corbis Sygma/Collart Herve: 30; Envision Stock Photography Inc.: 11 right (Steven Needham), 11 left (Paul Poplis); MapQuest.com, Inc.: 21; National Geographic Image Collection/Joel Sartore: 4 bottom; Peter Arnold Inc.: 33 (Herbert Giradet), 18 top (Michel Roggo), cover bottom right (Schafer & Hill), cover top left (Roland Seitre); Stone/Getty Images: 9 left (Daniel Bosler), 22, 23 left (Sylvain Grandadam), 23 right (Deborah Jaffe); Superstock, Inc.: 17; The Image Bank/Getty Images: 37 top (Peter Adams), 27 (Andy Caufield), cover center (Andrea Pistolesi), 5 top (Kevin Schafer), 6 top (Luis Viega); The Image Works: 28 bottom (John Babb/Professional Sports/Topham), 5 center (Tom Brakefield), 36 (Hinata Hata), 24 left (Sean Sprague).

Map by XNR Productions

Library of Congress Cataloging-in-Publication Data

Fontes, Justine.
  Brazil / by Justine and Ron Fontes.
      p. cm. – (A to Z)
Contents: Animals – Buildings – Cities – Dress – Exports – Food – Government – History – Important people – Jobs – Keepsakes – Land – Map – Nation – Only in Brazil – People – Question – Religion – School and sports – Transportation – Unusual Places – Visiting the Country – Window to the past – X-tra special things – Yearly festivals – Z – Let's Explore More.
Includes bibliographical references and index.
  ISBN 0-516-24563-5(lib. bdg.)   0-516-26806-6 (pbk.)
  1. Brazil–Juvenile literature. [1. Brazil.] I. Fontes, Ron. II. Title. III. Series.
  F2508.5.F59 2003
  981–dc21
                              2003005835

1 2 3 4 5 6 7 8 9 10 R 12 11 10 09 08 07 06 05 04 03

▪ Contents

Animals

Brazil is full of amazing animals, including many different kinds of monkeys, frogs, and birds. Many of Brazil's animals live in the huge Amazon **Rain Forest**.

Spider Monkey

Sloth

Anteaters eat mostly ants, but they can eat termites and other insects as well.

Sloths move very s-l-o-o-o-w-l-y. They spend their entire lives hanging from trees eating leaves and fruits, or sleeping.

Spider monkeys also live in trees, but they are much more active. They live in groups of up to 35 monkeys.

Rhinoceros beetles can carry up to 850 times their own weight! Male Rhinoceros beetles use their long horns to fight other beetles.

Brazil has many buildings with ultra-modern designs.

Buildings

For over 300 years, Brazil was a Portuguese colony. Many beautiful churches were built during that time. One of the most famous **colonial** churches is Igreja Sao Francisco de Assis in the city of Ouro Preto.

Brazil also has many modern buildings. Almost all the buildings in Brazil's capital, Brasilia, are modern.

Ouro Preto was named a Cultural Heritage of Mankind for its many colonial-era buildings.

Rio is one of the most unique cities in the world.

Cities

Sao Paulo is Brazil's biggest city, but Rio de Janeiro is its most famous. Known as Cidade Maravilhosa (Marvelous City) or simply "Rio," it has many famous beaches, including Copacabana and Ipanema.

Some of the richest and poorest Brazilians live in Rio. Luxury high-rises overlook its beaches, while slums called **favelas** surround the city.

Dress

Most Brazilians wear casual, modern clothing. Since Brazil is warm all year, people usually wear light clothes.

Vaqueiro

Brazilian women are very stylish. Girls often start wearing makeup and jewelry when they are young.

The state of Bahia was a slave-trading center during colonial times. Many of the people there descend from African slaves and still wear traditional African clothes. Women wear bright, long skirts and blouses, headscarves, and colorful necklaces and bracelets.

Brazil also has cowboys called **gauchos** and **vaqueiros**. Gauchos wear baggy pants called **bambachos** and ponchos. Vaqueiros wear leather chaps and hats.

Some of the most important car manufacturers in the world make their cars in Brazil.

This man is cutting sugarcane, which will be made into sugar.

Exports

There is a good chance something on your family's breakfast table came from Brazil. The country is one of the world's largest exporters of coffee, sugar, and oranges! Other important crops exported from Brazil are soybeans, nuts, and bananas.

Brazil also exports lots of steel and iron. Other important Brazilian exports are **manufactured** goods, like cars and other machinery.

Fried Plantains Recipe

WHAT YOU NEED:
- 2 plantains
- 1 tablespoon of butter or margarine
- Cinnamon and sugar to taste

HOW TO MAKE IT:
Peel the plantains and cut them in half lengthwise. Fry them in butter or margarine, first on one side, then on the other, until they are golden brown. Sprinkle with cinnamon and sugar to taste. Serve hot.

Food

Fried **plantains** is a popular dish in Brazil. They're eaten as a dessert, or as a side dish. Ask an adult to help you make some, using the recipe above.

Dom Pedro II

Government

Luis Inácio Lula da Silva became Brazil's president in January of 2003.

Brazilians aged 18 to 70 have to vote. Those who are 16, 17, or over 70 may vote if they want to. They elect a president for four years. A president can serve no more than two terms in a row. Brazilians also vote for the members of their Congress.

Dom Pedro II became king of Brazil in 1840, when he was only 15 years old! Pedro helped Brazil become more modern by building railroads, factories, and schools. In 1888, Pedro passed a law ending slavery in Brazil. The slave owners were so mad they made him give up his crown and leave the country. Today, Pedro II is a national hero.

The Portuguese brought slaves from Africa to work on their plantations. Brazil had over 3 million people.

This letter was written to the king of Portugal in 1500 announcing the discovery of Brazil by Pedro Alvarez Cabral.

History

When the Portuguese arrived in 1500, they built large **plantations** to grow sugarcane, cotton, and other crops. Brazilian rubber, gold, and diamonds made Portugal very rich.

Brazil became a republic in 1889, but for many years military dictators ruled the country. A dictator is someone who uses force to rule others.

Today, Brazil is a democracy, which means that the people elect their leaders.

13

Coffee by Candido Portinari, 1935

Important People

Candido Portinari's paintings are famous all over the world. He believed that art could help to better people's lives.

The Musicians by Candido Portinari, 1940-60

Candido Portinari was born in 1903 on a coffee plantation. He became famous for his paintings of the poor people of Brazil. Many of them show plantation workers and African descendents. Portinari wanted to show how difficult the lives of poor Brazilians really are.

His paintings and murals can be seen in Brazilian government buildings, the United States Library of Congress, and in the United Nations building in New York City. Portinari died in 1962.

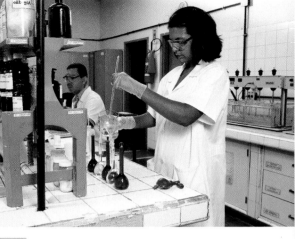

Pescador

(PESS-kah-dor)
means fisherman.

Jobs

Over half of the people in Brazil have service jobs. That means that they do things that help other people, like working for the government, in hospitals, schools, or stores.

Many Brazilians work in factories or mines. Others are farmers, gauchos, and fishermen. The Brazilian Rain Forest creates a lot of jobs too. Many plants are used to make medicines.

16

Wood carvings for sale

Keepsakes

Most Brazilian towns have markets where local people sell their crafts. You can find handmade pottery, baskets, leather goods, jewelry, and woodcarvings.

Carrancas are scary sculptures first made in the 1800s. They used to sit on the front of boats on the Sao Francisco River. The creatures were supposed to scare away "water monsters."

17

The Lateralis flower is just one of many
beautiful flowers that bloom in Brazil.

Land

Brazil is the fifth largest country in the
world. It is only slightly smaller than the
United States.

You can see the Amazon River from space!

The huge leaves, or pads, of the giant lily that grow in the Amazon are big enough to make a float for a child.

Brazil takes up almost half of South America. It borders every country in South America, except Chile and Ecuador. Brazil contains the world's largest rain forest. The Amazon Rain Forest is home to lots of wildlife, including over 25,000 different plants.

The Amazon River snakes through the rain forest. The Amazon is the second longest river in the world. It holds more water than the next three largest rivers combined!

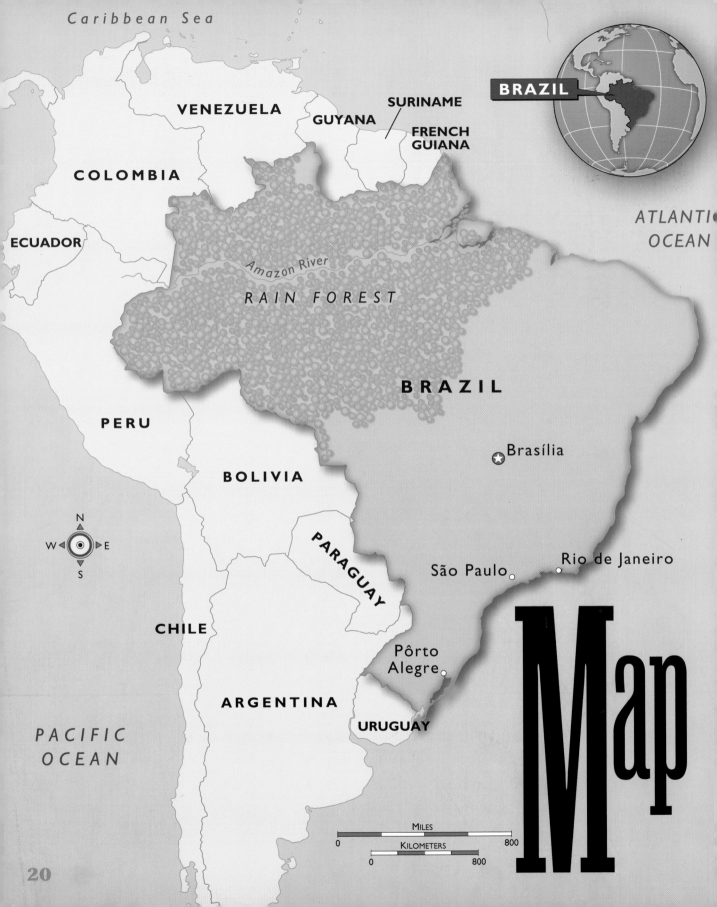

Caribbean Sea

VENEZUELA

GUYANA

SURINAME

FRENCH
GUIANA

COLOMBIA

ECUADOR

Amazon River

RAIN FOREST

BRAZIL

BRAZIL

PERU

Brasília

BOLIVIA

N

W   E

S

PARAGUAY

São Paulo

Rio de Janeiro

CHILE

ATLANTIC
OCEAN

Pôrto
Alegre

ARGENTINA

Map

URUGUAY

PACIFIC
OCEAN

MILES

0   800

KILOMETERS

0   800

Nation

In 1822, Brazil declared its independence from Portugal. At that time, the emperor of Brazil declared that the new nation's colors would no longer be the blue and white of Portugal, but green and yellow. The green stands for spring. The yellow stands for gold.

The stars in the Brazilian flag stand for the country's states. The white band across the flag's sky reads "Order and Progress."

Only in Brazil

Brazil is home to a unique mix of martial arts and dance known as **Capoeira**.

Capoeira is now practiced as a sport.

African slaves brought this style of foot-fighting, or kick boxing, to Brazil. Fearing violence, Brazilian masters told their slaves to stop practicing Capoeira. So the slaves disguised the martial art as a dance! Drums and tambourines often accompany Capoeira's graceful kicks.

People

Brazil is the largest Portuguese-speaking country in the world. Many Brazilians are of mixed origin, combining European and African ancestors. A small number of native tribes live in the Amazon jungle.

Brazilian families are very close. Most children live with their parents until they get married.

Most of Brazil's city dwellers live in modern apartment buildings. Almost a third of Brazilians live in slums called favelas. Favelas are full of crowded shacks that do not have electricity or running water.

People in rural areas live in small houses and often sleep in hammocks.

In the Amazon, families share a big, straw house called a **maloca**. Houses near rivers are raised on stilts to keep them dry.

Brazil's brave natives catch Piranha for their tasty meat. The Piranha's sharp teeth are used to make tools.

Question
What is a Piranha?

There are about 20 species of **piranha** living in Central and South America. Piranhas are small fish that travel in big numbers. Ranging from 6 inches (15 cm) to 2 feet (61 cm) long, piranhas sometimes swim in groups of several thousand.

Piranhas will bite anything that moves—even other piranhas. They have strong jaws and razor-sharp teeth. When a group finds a helpless animal, they quickly bite off its flesh. In minutes, even a beast as big as a horse can be chewed down to a skeleton!

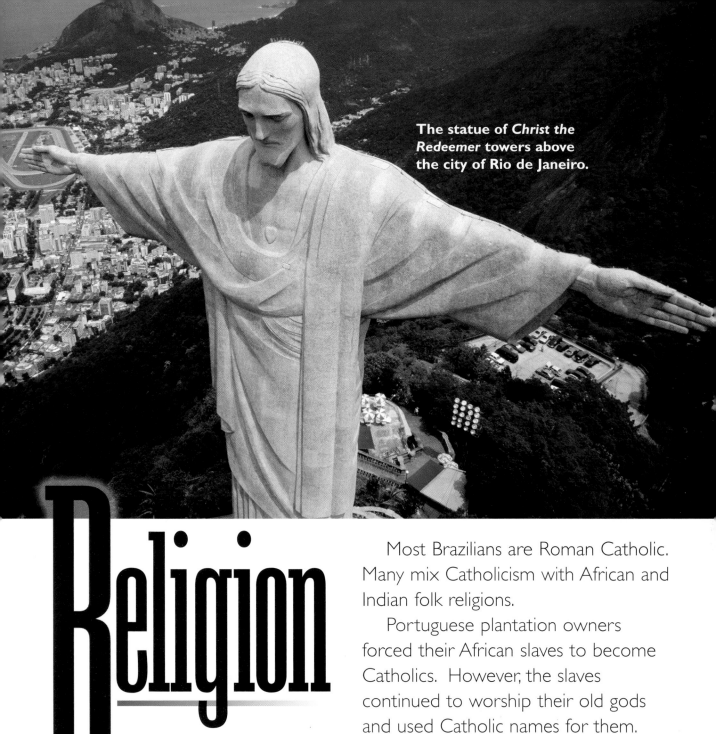

The statue of *Christ the Redeemer* towers above the city of Rio de Janeiro.

Religion

Most Brazilians are Roman Catholic. Many mix Catholicism with African and Indian folk religions.

Portuguese plantation owners forced their African slaves to become Catholics. However, the slaves continued to worship their old gods and used Catholic names for them.

Candomble and **Macumba** are two African religions that have mixed with the Catholic faith in Brazil. Believers drum and dance to get into a trance to contact spirits.

School & Sports

Brazil has free public schools. Children between the ages of 7 and 14 are required to attend school. Many poor children quit at 10 to start working. The government supports most colleges. Eighteen-year-olds must pass difficult exams in order to attend college for a low fee. Only about 1 out of 100 Brazilians go to college.

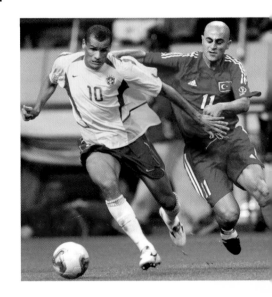

There are about 20,000 soccer teams in Brazil. It is the only country that has won the World Cup five times!

About one in ten Brazilians has a car. Almost half of those cars run on **ethanol.** This is a special fuel made from sugarcane. Most Brazilians travel by bus. In rural areas, some people still travel by horse, mule, or on foot.

In the Amazon, people travel by boats or canoes. The government has built large highways through some parts of the Amazon, but they usually flood during the rainy season.

More than 90 Brazilian cities have airports. The biggest airline in Brazil is called Varig.

Transportation

The Rio Negro (dark water) is the largest river in the world.

Unusual Places

The Amazon has two kinds of rivers: "black rivers" and "white rivers". "White rivers" are actually yellow or tan. Their waters are cloudy with dust called **silt**. The rushing streams wash silt off rocks and into rivers. "Black rivers" don't have silt because the streams that feed them flow over old rocks that have already been washed clean. Their waters are clear or dark.

Near the city of Manaus, the mighty Rio Negro flows into the muddy, yellow Amazon. The black river and the white river flow side by side in separate streams for many miles. Finally the waters swirl together and mix.

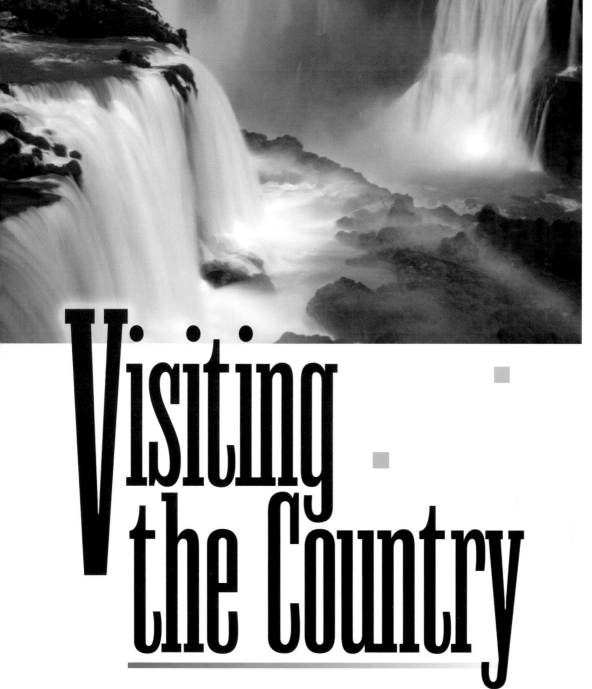

Visiting the Country

The Iguacu Falls are located in the border between Brazil, Paraguay, and Argentina, and they are huge! They are taller than Niagara Falls. The falls are over 2 miles (3.2 km) wide, and average 200 feet (61 m) high. They are made up of 275 different falls, or **cataracts**.

The falls are so unique that in 1986 they were declared a Natural Heritage of Mankind.

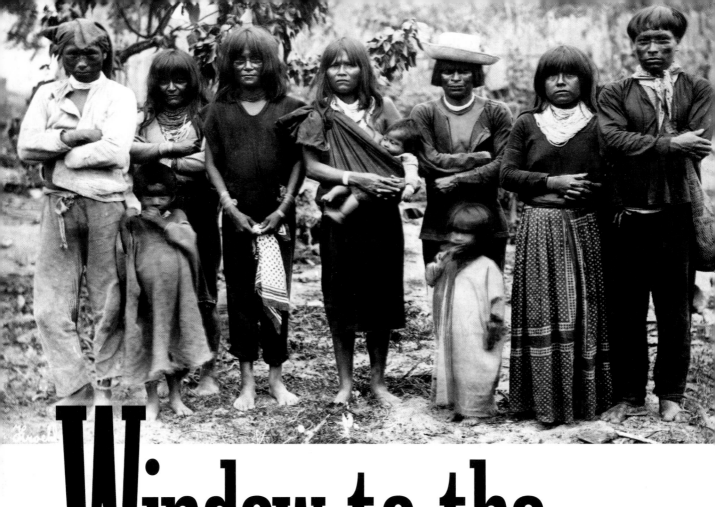

Window to the Past

When the Portuguese came to Brazil it was home to over 3 million Indians. Deep in the Amazon Rain Forest there are still tribes that have little contact with the modern world.

Over 200 different tribes live along the rivers in the Amazon Rain Forest. Each has its own customs and language.

Some fish or raise goats and other animals, others grow crops like beans and corn. Some tribes are hunters and gatherers. Gatherers find food, instead of growing crops. The Amazon tribes know a lot about the region's many plants and animals.

Although the Indians have survived, diseases have killed many of them. They have lost a lot of their land too.

Hairstyles, clothes, jewelry, body paints, and tattoos show what tribe the Indians belong to.

Canoes are a common form of transportation on the Amazon.

The trunk of the silk floss tree is covered with thick thorns.

X-tra Special Things

Scientists believe the Amazon Rain Forest produces one-third of the world's **oxygen**. Animals and people could not live without the oxygen in the air we breathe.

New kinds of logging are being developed to preserve the giant trees of the Amazon Rain Forest.

The black-headed sagui dwarf monkey is only 4 inches (10 cm) long!

The hairs on this caterpillar are poisonous!

Rain forests get at least 100 inches (2.5 m) of rain a year. Just a few miles of forest may have 1500 different kinds of flowers, 750 types of trees, 400 different bird species, and thousands of amazing insects. Native tribes use the plants as medicine. Many scientists think these plants might cure all kinds of diseases.

The giant trees of the rain forest filter huge amounts of air and water. As the trees are cut down for lumber and to clear land, the Earth's air and climate are changing. Almost half of Earth's rain forests are already gone. People all over the world are working to preserve what is left, like the Amazon.

Colorful floats line the streets in Rio de Janeiro during Carnaval.

Yearly Festivals

Brazil's most famous festival is **Carnaval**. People flock to Rio to see one of the most amazing parades in the world.

Music is an important part of celebrating Brazil's Independence Day.

For a week in late February or early March, Brazil throws a huge party. Carnaval starts on the Sunday before the Catholic holiday of **Lent**. Brazilians dress in colorful costumes and dance in the streets. In Rio, the 26 best **samba** schools compete. The schools are neighborhood groups that spend all year making floats and costumes, and practicing their dances.

On September 7, 1822, Brazil went from being a Portuguese colony to an independent country. Like July 4 in the United States, Independence Day is a national holiday in Brazil.

On All Soul's Day, November 2, Brazilians visit the graves of lost loved ones. They bring flowers and candles, and say prayers for those who are gone but not forgotten.

Zarpar

Pedro Alvarez Cabral

Navio

(NUH-vee-oh) means ship.

Zarpar means to set sail. Between 1420 and 1620, Europeans set out in ships to find spices, gold, and other valuable things. Back then, much of the Earth had not yet been mapped. Ships were at the mercy of the weather.

When Admiral Pedro Alvarez Cabral set sail from Lisbon, Portugal, in 1500, he was headed for India. Six weeks later, he was surprised to find the land now known as Brazil. No one is sure why Cabral's 13 ships were so far away, but this changed the course of Brazil's history!

Portuguese and English Words

bambachos (bahm-BAH-choss) baggy pants worn by Brazilian cowboys

bandeira (ban-DAY-rah) flag

Candomble (kahn-DOME-bleh) an Afro-Brazilian religion

capoeira (kah-poo-AY-rah) a Brazilian mix of martial arts and dance

Carnaval (KAR-nuh-vuhl) a week-long party that starts on the Sunday before Lent

carrancas (kah-RRANG-kahs) wooden carvings originally made to scare water monsters away from boats

cataract (KAT-uh-rakt) a tall waterfall

colonial (kuh-LOH-nee-uhl) a period of time when people left their homes to settle in a new place

ethanol (EE-theh-nawl) grain alcohol, a clean-burning fuel made from plants

favela (fah-VEH-lah) a slum; an overcrowded, poor neighborhood

gaucho (GOU-choh) a South American cowboy

Guarani (guah-rah-NEE) one of the Amazon tribes

Lent (lent) 40 weekdays before Easter during which many Catholics give up meat and other pleasures

Macumba (mah-KOOM-bah) voodoo; religious witchcraft

maloca (mah-LOH-kah) a large straw house shared by one or more Amazon tribal families

manufactured (man-yuh-FAK-churd) something that has been made, usually with machines in a factory

navio (NUH-vee-oh) ship

oxygen (OK-suh-juhn) a colorless, tasteless, odorless gas found in air, water, and many other substances that animals breathe to live

piranha (per-AH-nuh) small, South American fish with extremely sharp teeth

plantain (PLAN-tuhn) a tropical fruit like a banana, but not as sweet and usually eaten cooked

plantation (plan-TAY-shuhn) a large farm

rain forest (raynFOR-ist) a thick, tropical forest with heavy rainfall

samba (SAHM-bah) a Brazilian dance originally from Africa

silt (silt) fine particles of soil washed by flowing water into a river or lake

vaqueiro (vah-kee-AY-roh) cowboy

Let's Explore More

Carnaval by George Ancona, Harcourt, 1999

Count Your Way Through Brazil (Count Your Way) by James Haskins, Carolrhoda Books, 1996

Brazil (Festivals of the World) by Susan McKay, Gareth Stevens, 1997

Websites

www.brasilemb.org/kids1.shtml
Learn about Brazilian children, animals, native people; visit Brasilia, and much more on this Brazilian Embassy website.

www.amazonrainforest.org/kidfun/kidfun.asp
Find out how to help save the rainforest; enjoy games, stories, contests, and links to other sites.

http://www.d23.org/sullivan/travis/Explorer%20Book/Cabral.htm
Read more about Pedro Alvares Cabral, the Portuguese explorer that discovered Brazil.

Index

Italic page numbers indicate illustrations

Meet the Authors

JUSTINE & RON FONTES have written nearly 400 children's books together. Since 1988, they have published *critter news*, a free newsletter that keeps them in touch with publishers from their home in Maine.

The Fonteses have written many biographies and early readers, as well as historical novels and other books combining facts with stories. Their love of animals is expressed in the nature notes columns of *critter news*.

During his childhood in Tennessee, Ron was a member of the Junior Classical League and went on to tutor Latin students. At 16, Ron was drawing a science fiction comic strip for the local newspaper. A professional artist for 30 years, Ron has also been in theater as a costumer, makeup artist, and designer.

Justine was born in New York City and worked in publishing while earning a BA in English Literature Phi Beta Kappa from New York University. Thanks to her parents' love of travel, Justine visited most of Europe as a child, going as far north as Finland. During college, she spent time in France and Spain.